DARE YOU NOT TO LAUGH

Great Clean Jokes for Kids

DARE YOU Not ^ TO LAUGH

Great Clean Jokes for Kids

BARBOUR **kidz**

A Division of Barbour Publishing

© 2021 by Barbour Publishing, Inc.

Compiled by Jennifer Hahn

Print ISBN 978-1-64352-799-4

All rights reserved. No part of this publication may be reproduced or transmitted for commercial purposes, except for brief quotations in printed reviews, without written permission of the publisher.

Churches and other noncommercial interests may reproduce portions of this book without the express written permission of Barbour Publishing, provided that the text does not exceed 500 words and that the text is not material quoted from another publisher. When reproducing text from this book, include the following credit line: "From *Dare You Not to Laugh: Great Clean Jokes for Kids*, published by Barbour Publishing, Inc. Used by permission."

Scripture taken from the HOLY BIBLE, NEW INTERNATIONAL VERSION®. NIV®. Copyright © 1973, 1978, 1984, 2011 by Biblica, Inc.™ Used by permission. All rights reserved worldwide.

Published by Barbour Publishing, Inc., 1810 Barbour Drive, Uhrichsville, Ohio 44683, www.barbourbooks.com

Our mission is to inspire the world with the life-changing message of the Bible.

ⓔⓒⓟⓐ Member of the
Evangelical Christian
Publishers Association

Printed in the United States of America.
000706 0321 BP

CONTENTS

· ·

INTRODUCTION:
DARE YOU NOT TO LAUGH!

Worried mom: My son thinks he's a dog. He barks at people and chases cats.

Doctor: Hmm. . . . How long has he behaved like this?

Mom: Since he was a puppy.

Did you know that the Bible says "a cheerful heart is good medicine" (Proverbs 17:22)? Well, here's a healthy dose for kids ages eight to twelve.

Dare You Not to Laugh: Great Clean Jokes for Kids is jam-packed with jokes on school and church, sports and the outdoors, family and food, technology and transportation, you name it.

They're clean! They're funny! We dare you not to laugh! We Double Dog Dare you—even Triple Dog Dare you—on some of them!

1.
SCRIPTURAL SNICKERS

How many animals did Moses take on the ark?

Moses didn't take any animals on the ark. Noah did.

Why didn't Noah fish much?

He only had two worms.

What did the well-mannered sheep say to the other animals waiting to get on the ark?

"After ewe!"

What did Noah say to the frogs?

"Hop on in!"

Who spent most of their time on their knees in the ark?

The birds of pray.

After the flood, why didn't some of the snakes "go forth and multiply"?

They couldn't—they were adders.

What was Noah's profession?

He was an ark-itect.

Was Noah the first out of the ark?

No, he came forth out of the ark.

What did Noah say as he was loading the ark?

"Now I herd everything."

Why didn't anyone play cards on the ark?

Because Noah sat on the deck.

Which animals did Noah distrust?

The cheetahs.

What kind of light did Noah have on the ark?

Floodlights.

Which animals were the last to leave the ark?

The elephants. It took time for them to pack their trunks.

DOUBLE DOG DARE

What kind of man was Boaz before he married?

Ruthless.

How did Jonah feel when the whale swallowed him?

Down in the mouth.

How long did Cain dislike his brother?

As long as he was Abel.

Who was the first tennis player in the Bible?

Joseph—he served in Pharaoh's court.

Who was the fastest runner in history?
Adam. He was first in the human
race.

Who was the shortest man in the Bible?
Knee-high-miah (Nehemiah).

What season was it when Eve ate the
fruit?
Early in the fall.

DOUBLE DOG DARE

**Which Bible character had
no parents?**
Joshua. He was the son
of Nun.

What do people today have that Adam
didn't?
Ancestors.

What time of day was Adam created?
Just a little before Eve.

What's the first court case mentioned in the Bible?
Joshua Judges Ruth.

TRIPLE DOG DARE

Which part of Israel was especially wealthy?
The Jordan River.
The banks were always overflowing.

When is baseball first mentioned in the Bible?
Genesis 1:1—"In the big inning. . ."

What was the first medication in the Bible?
When God gave Moses two tablets.

Why didn't Samson want to argue with Delilah?

He didn't want to split hairs.

How do we know Peter was a wealthy fisherman?

Because of his net income.

Where was Solomon's temple located?

On the side of his head.

TRIPLE DOG DARE

Who was the most intelligent man in the Bible?
Abraham, because he knew a Lot.

2.
I SMELL A RAT...OR A BAT...
OR A CAT...OR A GNAT

How does an octopus go into battle?
Fully armed.

What did the boy octopus say to the girl octopus?
"I want to hold your hand, hand, hand, hand, hand, hand, hand, hand."

First octopus: What do you like least about being an octopus?
Second octopus: Washing my hands before dinner.

What does an octopus wear when it is cold?
A coat of arms.

What kind of key opens a banana?
A mon-key.

What do you call two octopi who look exactly alike?
Itentacle.

What animals have keys but can't open locks?
Monkeys, turkeys, and donkeys.

A tourist was on an excursion through the swamps of Florida. "Is it true that alligators won't attack you as long as you're carrying a flashlight?" he asked.
The guide answered, "Well, that depends on how fast you carry the flashlight."

What's black and white and red all over?
A blushing zebra.

What has stripes and goes around and around?
A zebra in a revolving door.

"You boys! Stop that!" yelled the zookeeper. He hurried over to the group. "You are scaring the animals! Tell me your names and what you were doing." The boys lowered their heads and began their confessions.

"My name is George," said the first boy, "and I threw peanuts into the elephant pen."

"My name is Larry," said the second boy, "and I threw peanuts into the elephant pen."

"My name is Mike," said the third boy, "and I threw peanuts into the elephant pen."

"My name is Peanuts," said the fourth boy.

What did the zookeeper like to snack on?
    Animal crackers.

How did the zookeeper catch the escaped cat?
    The leopard was spotted.

What does a caterpillar do at the beginning of each year?
    She turns over a new leaf.

What do cats like to read?
    Mews-papers.

Why are cats such bad storytellers?
    They only have one tale.

What is noisier than a cat stuck in a tree?
    Two cats stuck in a tree.

How did the cat bake a cake?
    From scratch.

Where does a cat go when he loses his tail?

A retail store.

What did the cat get on the test?

A purr-fect score.

DOUBLE DOG DARE

What do you call a cat that climbed in a dryer?

Fluffy.

What's the difference between a cat and a comma?

A cat has its claws at the end of its paws; a comma is a pause at the end of a clause.

Ten cats were on a boat and one jumped off. How many were left?

None—they were all copycats.

Why did the family of cats move next door to the family of mice?
    So they could have the neighbors for dinner.

What happened when the lion ate the comedian?
    He felt funny.

How many lions can you fit into an empty cage?
    One. After that, it isn't empty anymore.

What does the lion say to his friends before they go out hunting?
    "Let us prey."

How does a leopard change its spots?
    When he gets tired of one spot, he moves to another.

What do fashionable frogs wear in the spring?
    Open-toad sandals.

Why do giraffes have such small appetites?

Because with them, a little goes a long way.

What do you call a story told by a giraffe?

A tall tale.

Why did the giraffe graduate early?

She was head and shoulders above the rest of her class.

Why won't banks allow kangaroos to open accounts?

Their checks always bounce.

What is the best year for a kangaroo?

Leap year.

Why does a mother kangaroo hope it doesn't rain?

She doesn't like it when the kids have to play inside.

Why do porcupines always win games?
   They finish with the most points.

Why did the turtle go to a counselor?
   He wanted to come out of his shell.

Why did the rock band hire a chicken?
   They needed the drumsticks.

How did the young turtle contact his parents?
   He used his shell phone.

Why did Mozart sell his chickens?
   They kept saying, "Bach, Bach, Bach."

TRIPLE DOG DARE

 What's the best way to catch a squirrel?
   Climb a tree and act like a nut.

What do you call two spiders that just married?

Newlywebs.

Two hens were pecking in the yard when suddenly a softball sailed over the fence and landed a few feet away. One hen said to the other, "Look at the eggs they're turning out next door!"

Why do spiders make the best baseball players?

They are known for catching flies.

What do you get if you feed gunpowder to a chicken?

An eggs-plosion.

If a rooster laid an egg on the top of a roof, which side of the roof would the egg roll down?

Neither. Roosters don't lay eggs.

What side of a chicken has the most feathers?
    The outside.

What day of the week do chickens dread?
    Fry-day.

Why did the chicken cross the road?
    To show the opossum it could be done.

Why won't clams lend you money?
    Because they are shellfish.

DOUBLE DOG DARE

What do you call a fish with no eye?
    Fsh.

Why are fish afraid to play volleyball?
    They might get caught in the net.

What shellfish likes to lift weights?
    Mussels.

What animal is always thinking about its weight?
    A fish. He carries his scales around with him.

What kind of money do crabs use?
    Sand dollars.

Why are rabbits so good at math?
    They love to multiply.

What do rabbits put on the back of their cars?
    Thumper stickers.

What did the pink rabbit say to the blue rabbit?
    "Cheer up!"

How do you know that carrots are good for your eyes?

Have you ever seen a rabbit wearing glasses?

How do you catch a unique rabbit?

Unique up on it.

How do you catch a tame rabbit?

Tame way. Unique up on it.

If baby pigs are called piglets, why aren't baby bulls called bullets and baby chickens chicklets?

What is worse than a giraffe with a sore neck?

A centipede with itchy feet.

A turtle was mugged by three snails, but when a police officer asked the turtle to give a description of what happened, all he could say was, "I don't know, officer. It all happened so fast!"

What do you get when you cross a dog with an elephant?

A very nervous mail carrier.

What do you get when you cross an elephant with a kangaroo?

Big holes all over Australia.

TRIPLE DOG DARE

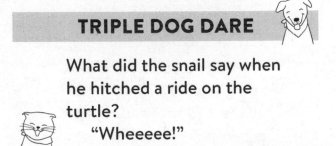

What did the snail say when he hitched a ride on the turtle?

"Wheeeee!"

Little Tommy suddenly found himself surrounded by thirty galloping horses, twenty-five charging bears, and ten roaring lions. How did he survive?

He got off the merry-go-round.

What do you get when you cross a hen with a hyena?

An animal that laughs at every yolk.

What do you get when you cross a pig and a centipede?

Bacon and legs.

DOUBLE DOG DARE

Frank: Did you hear about the guy who was arrested at the zoo for feeding the pigeons?

Harry: No. What's wrong with feeding the pigeons?

Frank: He fed them to the lions.

What should you do when someone throws a goose at you?

Duck.

What do you say when someone throws a duck at another duck?

"Duck, duck!"

What do you say when someone throws a goose at a duck?

"Duck, duck! Goose!"

What grows up while it grows down?

A duckling.

What does a skunk use to defend itself?

In-stinkt.

How does a skunk's car run?

On fumes.

How many skunks does it take to smell up a neighborhood?

Just a phew.

What animal is the strongest?

A snail. He carries his house with him.

What was the snail doing on the highway?

About a mile a week.

Ben was watching his favorite television show when someone knocked on his door. Grumpily, Ben got up and opened the door only to find a snail collecting money for charity.

"You made me miss my show for that?" Ben grumbled. Then he gave the snail a big kick.

A year later, Ben was watching television and heard a knock at the door.

He opened the door to find the same snail there, looking dejected. "What was that all about?" the creature asked.

What would you call a snake that drinks too much coffee?

A hyper viper.

Why can't you play a joke on a snake?

Because you can't pull their legs.

What kind of snake is good at math?

An adder.

What school subject are snakes best at?

Hiss-tory.

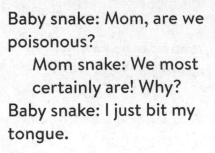

TRIPLE DOG DARE

Baby snake: Mom, are we poisonous?

Mom snake: We most certainly are! Why?

Baby snake: I just bit my tongue.

What do you call a cow with two legs?
    Lean beef.

What do you call a cow with no legs?
    Ground beef.

What did the horse say after it tripped?
    "Help, I've fallen and I can't
    giddyup!"

What do you call a cow that has just
given birth?
    De-calfinated.

What is cowhide used for?
    Holding cows together.

What goes *tick-tock woof-woof*?
    A watchdog.

What do you call a sleeping bull?
    A bulldozer.

Which is richer, a bull or a cow?
A bull. The cow gives you milk; the
bull charges you.

What newspaper did the dinosaurs
prefer?
The *Prehistoric Times*.

What do you call a blind dinosaur?
Do-you-think-he-saurus.

What wears a coat all winter and pants
in the summer?
A dog.

How does a dog stop the DVD player?
He presses the Paws button.

Have you heard about the dog that ate
an onion?
His bark was much worse than his
bite.

How are dogs like phones?
    They have collar IDs.

What did the hungry dalmatian say after he'd eaten?
    "That hit the spots."

Where do dogs like to go river rafting?
    In Collie-rado.

Man: Are you certain this dog you're selling me is loyal?
    Owner: Of course he is. I've sold him five times, and every time he's come back.

What do you get when you cross Lassie with a petunia?
    A collie flower.

Where do little dogs sleep when they go camping?
    In pup tents.

DOUBLE DOG DARE

"Why is your dog growling at me while I'm eating?" Dave asked Steve. "Does he want me to give him some food?"

"No," said Steve. "He's just mad because you're eating off his favorite plate."

What is as big as a hippopotamus but weighs nothing at all?
    The hippo's shadow.

What did the donkey send out at Christmastime?
    Mule-tide greetings.

What is an owl's favorite mystery?
    A whoo-dunit.

A man entered a country store and noticed a sign reading DANGER! BEWARE OF DOG posted on the glass door.

Inside, a harmless old hound dog was asleep on the floor beside the counter. He asked the store owner, "Is that the dog folks are supposed to beware of?"

"Yup, sure is," the owner replied.

The stranger couldn't help but smile in amusement. "That certainly doesn't appear to be a dangerous dog to me. Why did you post that sign?"

"Well," he replied, "before I posted that sign, people kept tripping over him."

TRIPLE DOG DARE

What do you call a penguin in the desert?
Lost.

A man had just gotten two new dogs and wanted his mother to see them. So he invited her over for a meal.

As Mom sat at the table, she noticed that the dishes were dirty. "Have these plates been washed?" she asked.

"They're as clean as soap and water could get them," the son answered. She wasn't convinced but started eating anyway. Despite the appearance of the dishes, the food was delicious.

When dinner was over, the man took the plates and set them on the floor. Then he whistled and yelled, "Here, Soap! Here, Water!"

How did the owl with laryngitis feel?
    He didn't give a hoot.

What does an educated owl say?
    "Whom."

What is black and white and keeps going in a circle?

A penguin in a revolving door.

What is a pig's favorite play?

Hamlet.

What do you get when you cross a pig and a tree?

A porky pine.

How do pigs say goodbye?

With hogs and kisses.

What do you call a pig doing karate?

A pork chop.

Why shouldn't you tell a secret to a pig?

He's a squealer.

How did the farmer's baseball team win the game?

The last little piggy ran all the way home.

Why was the pig kicked off the soccer team?

He hogged the ball.

Why did the otter cross the road?

To get to the otter side.

Why did the weasel cross the road twice?

He was a double-crosser.

What did daddy buffalo say to his boy as he was leaving?

"Bison."

What kind of ant is good at math?

An account-ant.

How does a beaver know which tree to cut down?

Whichever one he chews.

What is a shark's favorite game?

Swallow the Leader.

How do you get the attention of a sheep?

Yell, "Hey, ewe!"

What do you call a hundred-year-old ant?

An ant-ique.

Why was the baby ant confused?

Because all his uncles were ants.

What happened when the frog's car broke down?

He couldn't get it jumped, so he needed to have it toad.

What do you call a grizzly bear with no teeth?

A gummy bear.

How do bears walk around?

In bear feet.

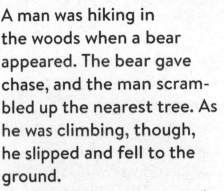

A man was hiking in the woods when a bear appeared. The bear gave chase, and the man scrambled up the nearest tree. As he was climbing, though, he slipped and fell to the ground.

"Lord," the man prayed, "please let this be a Christian bear."

And the bear said, "Heavenly Father, I thank Thee for this food."

Where do polar bears vote?
   The North Poll.

What did the teddy bear say when he was offered dessert?
   "No thanks, I'm stuffed."

What vegetable do you get when an elephant walks through your garden?
    Squash.

Two guys were hiking in the forest when they suddenly came across a big grizzly bear. One man quickly removed his hiking boots and put on running shoes. His friend said, "You're crazy! Don't you know how fast grizzlies are? You'll never outrun him!"
    "Outrun the bear?" the man replied, "I only have to outrun *you*!"

Why are elephants cheaper to hire than other animals?
    They work for peanuts.

What time is it when an elephant sits on your fence?
    Time to get a new fence.

What did the bee say to his barber?
    "Just give me a buzz, please."

Why are elephants known to hold grudges?

They can forgive, but they can't forget.

What kind of bee is always dropping the football?

A fumble-bee.

What did Mr. Bee say when he arrived home to his wife?

"Hi, honey."

Have you heard the story about the peacock that crossed the road?

It really is a colorful tale. . . .

What kind of dancing do woodpeckers prefer?

Tap dancing.

Why do hummingbirds hum?

They can never remember the words to the song.

What kind of bird shows up at every meal?

A swallow.

Matt: How did your parakeet die?
Herb: Flu.
Matt: Parakeets can't die from the flu.
Herb: Mine did. She flew under a bus.

What kept the performing pony from singing?

It was a little horse.

Why did the pony get in trouble?

She just wouldn't stop horsing around.

A man rode into town on Monday, stayed five days, and then rode out on Monday. How is this possible?

His horse was named Monday.

What is the loudest pet?

A trum-pet.

A man from the city visited a ranch. He was talking with the ranch hand. "I finally went for a ride this morning."

The ranch hand asked, "Horseback?"

"Yep," the man replied. "He got back about an hour before I did."

3.
WORKIN' FOR A LIVIN', LIVIN' AND A WORKIN'

. . . .

How did the salesman call his client?
    He used the sell phone.

Which workers are best at communication?
    Fishermen. They're always dropping a line.

Why are electricians the most informed people?
    They keep up with current events.

Why was the car mechanic fired?
    He took too many brakes.

What did the chef say to the boiling water as he left the kitchen?
    "You will be mist."

Why can't scientists trust atoms?
   Because they make up everything.

Why did the man become an
archaeologist?
   Because his career was in ruins.

Why did the invisible man turn down a
job offer?
   He really couldn't see himself
   working there.

DOUBLE DOG DARE

What training do you need
to be a garbage collector?
   None. You just pick it up
   as you go along.

How did the scientist invent bug spray?
   She started from scratch.

Did you hear about the man who invented breath fresheners?
Word is that he made a mint.

Why is April the accountant's least favorite month?
It's just too taxing.

TRIPLE DOG DARE

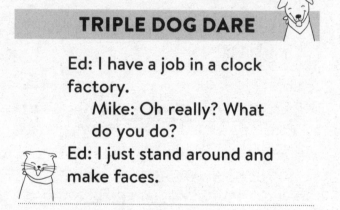

Ed: I have a job in a clock factory.
Mike: Oh really? What do you do?
Ed: I just stand around and make faces.

What is a chiropractor's favorite music?
Hip-pop.

What do you need to know to be an auctioneer?
Lots.

Two gas company servicemen were checking meters in a neighborhood. They parked their truck at one end of an alley and worked their way to the other end. At the last house, the owner watched out her kitchen window as they checked her meter.

As the servicemen finished, the older one challenged his younger coworker to a footrace back to their truck.

As they reached their vehicle, they realized someone was running up right behind them. "What's wrong?" they asked the woman. In between breaths, she explained, "When I saw the two of you check my meter then take off running, I figured I'd better run too!"

A man at a construction site was bragging he was stronger than anyone. He began making fun of an older workmen. After awhile, the older worker had enough.

"I'll bet I can haul something over to that other building that you won't be able to wheel back."

"Okay," the young man replied. "Let's see what you've got."

The older man reached out and grabbed a wheelbarrow by the handles. Then he looked at the young man and said with a smile, "All right. Get in."

A store manager overheard one of his salesmen talking to a customer. "No, sir," said the salesman. "We haven't had any for a while, and it doesn't look like we'll be getting any soon."

The manager immediately called the salesman over to him. "Don't you ever tell a customer we're out of anything! Now, what did he want?"

"Rain," answered the salesman.

What is the fastest way to annoy a doctor?

Take away his patients.

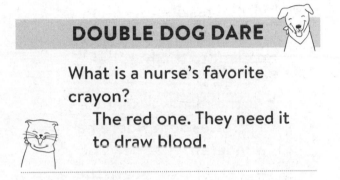

DOUBLE DOG DARE

What is a nurse's favorite crayon?

The red one. They need it to draw blood.

A new nurse listened while the doctor was yelling, "Typhoid! Tetanus! Measles!"

"Why is he doing that?" she asked another nurse.

"Oh, he just likes to call the shots around here," she replied.

I told the doctor I kept hearing a buzzing sound, but she told me it was just a bug going around.

TRIPLE DOG DARE

A man returned from an overseas trip very ill. He visited his doctor, who immediately sent the patient to the hospital for tests.

The man was sent to a private room where he wondered what news he would receive. Soon, the phone by his bed rang.

"Hello, this is your doctor," the voice on the line said. "We have the results from your tests, and it seems you have an extremely contagious virus."

"Oh no!" the man replied. "What are you going to do?"

"Well," said the doctor, "we're going to put you →

on a diet of pizzas and pancakes."

"Pizzas and pancakes?" the man repeated. "And that will cure me?"

"Well, no," the doctor answered, "but it's the only food we can slide under your door."

Sydney: I must have sneezed fifty times today. Do you think there's something in the air?

Matt: Yes—your germs!

Doctor: How is the boy who swallowed the quarter?

Nurse: No change yet.

Patient: Doctor, Doctor! I think I swallowed a spoon!

Doctor: Just sit quietly and try not to stir.

A young woman went to her doctor, complaining of pain. "Where are you hurting?" asked the doctor.

"I hurt all over," said the woman.

"Can you be a little more specific?"

The woman touched her right knee with her index finger and yelled, "Ow, that hurts." Then she touched her left cheek and yelled, "Ouch! That hurts too." Then she touched her right earlobe. "Ow, even that hurts!" she cried.

The doctor examined her for a moment then reported his diagnosis. "Ma'am, you have a broken finger."

A man went to the doctor and said, "Doc, every time I drink coffee, I get terrible pains in my eye."

The doctor said, "Next time, take the spoon out of your cup."

A man arrived at the emergency room with both of his ears badly burned. "How did this happen?" the doctor asked. →

"I was ironing my shirt when the phone rang, and I answered the iron by mistake," explained the man.

"Well, what about the other ear?" the doctor inquired.

"That happened when I called for the ambulance."

Farmer Brown: Did you lose much in that last tornado?

Farmer Jones: Lost the henhouse and all the chickens. But that was all right—I ended up with three new cows and somebody's pickup truck.

Farmer: Quite a storm we had last night.

Neighbor: Yep, it sure was.

Farmer: Did it damage your barn any?

Neighbor: I dunno. I haven't found it yet.

DOUBLE DOG DARE

A woman was frantic when she saw smoke coming from her garage. She called 911 to report the fire. "How do we get there?" asked the emergency dispatcher.

"Well. . . ," the woman said, "don't they use those big red trucks anymore?"

Several fire departments were called to the scene of a large blaze. One particular truck sped through the streets of the city, arriving well ahead of the others. Its crew was later recognized for their dedication to the job.

At a dinner given in the firemen's honor, the mayor gave a speech saying their incredibly fast response had helped save both the building and the people inside. "What can we give you →

to show our gratitude for your work?"
asked the mayor. "New brakes," one
fireman replied.

City man, to farmer: Lived here all your
life?
    Farmer: Not yet.

How did the rancher prepare for each
season?
    By making long-range plans.

Why did the farmer receive an award?
    Because he was outstanding in his
    field.

Did you hear about the woman who
gave up gardening?
    She just threw in the trowel.

Why did the man get fired from the
calendar factory?
    He took a couple days off.

Employer: I thought you requested yesterday afternoon off to go see your dentist.

Employee: Yes, sir.

Employer: Then why did I see you coming out of the baseball stadium with a friend?

Employee: That was my dentist.

Why did the carpenter quit his job?
He was board.

A man got a job in road maintenance, painting the yellow lines in the middle of the highway. On the third day, the supervisor called the new employee into his office. "The first day, you painted three miles of highway, the second day one mile, and today you only painted one hundred yards," he complained. "Why do you keep slowing down?"

"I'm doing the best I can," the man answered. "I just keep getting farther away from the paint can!"

Janelle was looking for a new job. She emailed dozens of companies and attached her résumé each time.

Three weeks later, she was wondering why she had not received even one request for an interview.

Finally she received a message from a prospective employer that explained the problem. It read: "Your résumé was not attached as you stated it would be. But the photo of the beach was beautiful!"

A man was interviewing for a job. "And remember," said the interviewer, "we are very strict about cleanliness. Did you wipe your shoes on the mat before entering?"

"Oh, yes, sir," replied the man.

The interviewer narrowed his eyes and said, "We are also very strict about honesty. There is no mat."

DOUBLE DOG DARE

The owner of a factory decided to make a surprise visit and check up on his staff. As he walked through the plant, he noticed a young man doing nothing but leaning against a wall. The businessman marched up to the young man and said angrily, "How much do you make a week?"

"Three hundred dollars, sir," replied the young man.

Whipping out his wallet, the company owner removed three hundred dollars, shoved it into the young man's hands, and said, "Here is a week's pay— now get out and don't come back!"

Turning to one of the →

supervisors, the owner asked, "Just how long has that lazy kid been working here?"

"Oh, he doesn't work here," said the supervisor.  "He was just here delivering our pizzas."

Why are carpenters in charge of building contracts?
They like to hammer out all the details.

How did the carpenter use only one brick to finish building a house?
It was the last one.

If a gardener has a green thumb and bankers have gold thumbs, who has a black-and-blue thumb?
A carpenter.

How did the carpenter break his teeth?
　　He chewed his nails.

What is the rank of a dentist in the Marines?
　　Drill sergeant.

What do you call a scientist whose life is in ruins?
　　An archaeologist.

DOUBLE DOG DARE

Did you hear about the accident at the upholstery factory?
　　All is fine now. The employee is fully recovered.

What is an astronaut's favorite meal?
　　Launch.

What is the best way to put a baby astronaut to bed?

You rock-et.

Why did the astronaut keep changing his course?

He didn't take the time to plan-et!

What part of the keyboard do astronauts like best?

The space bar.

One astronaut asks another if he has heard of the planet Saturn.

The second astronaut says, "I'm not sure, but it has a familiar ring."

If athletes get athlete's foot, what do astronauts get?

Missile-toe.

A young executive was preparing to leave the office late one evening when he found the company owner standing in front of a paper shredder with a document in his hand.

"This is a very sensitive and important document," said the boss, "and my secretary has gone for the night. Can you get this thing to work for me?"

"Certainly," said the young executive eagerly. He turned the machine on, inserted the paper, and pressed the START button.

"Excellent! Thank you!" said the CEO as his paper disappeared inside the machine. "I just need one copy...."

What did the astronaut think of the takeoff?

It was a blast.

Why did the sailor have trouble learning the alphabet?

He always got lost at C.

What did the drummer name his twin daughters?

Anna 1, Anna 2.

4.
TELL ME A STORY, READ ME A BOOK

How do you get to "Once Upon a Time" land?

Take the fairy boat.

Why wasn't Cinderella good at sports?

Because she had a pumpkin as her coach.

Why did Cinderella get thrown off the baseball team?

Because she ran away from the ball.

What did Cinderella call the cat who helped her get to the ball?

"My furry godmother."

Where do mermaids sleep?

In a water bed.

What did the Gingerbread Man use to fasten his vest?

Gingersnaps.

What fishing technique do the Three Billy Goats Gruff use?

Trolling.

DOUBLE DOG DARE

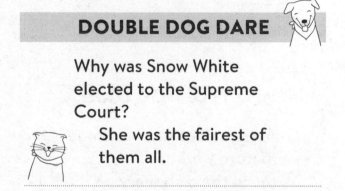

Why was Snow White elected to the Supreme Court?

She was the fairest of them all.

When all of the storybook princesses ran a race, who won?

Rapunzel, by a hair.

Why do dragons sleep during the day?

So they can hunt knights.

How did Rapunzel find her missing hairbrush?

She combed the land.

What did King Arthur like to sleep in?

A knightgown.

What magic reptile lives in the Emerald City?

The Lizard of Oz.

DOUBLE DOG DARE

Where does success come before work?

In the dictionary.

Did you hear the joke about the paper?

It really isn't that great. In fact, it's tearable.

Who wrote *I Love School*?
    I. M. Kidding.

Who wrote *America's Longest River*?
    Misses Sippy.

Who wrote *French Overpopulation*?
    Francis Crowded.

Who wrote *The Color of Eggs*?
    Summer Brown.

Who wrote *Lost in the Forest*?
    Miss Sing.

Who wrote *I Can Fly*?
    Ima Byrd.

Who wrote *How to Run a Successful Service Station*?
    Philip McCarr.

Who wrote *The New Shoes*?
    Ben Down and Ty Laces.

Who wrote *The Haunted Mansion*?
    Hugo First.

Who wrote *The World's Softest Toys*?
    Ted E. Bear.

Who wrote *How to Stay Home from School*?
    Fay King.

Who wrote *Parachuting Made Easy*?
    Will E. Maykit.

Who wrote *Plane Assembly*?
    Upton Away.

DOUBLE DOG DARE

Who wrote *How to Cook Wild Game*?
    Chris P. Duck.

Who wrote *The Long Walk Home*?
   Miss D. Buss.

Who wrote *Guide to European Sports Cars*?
   Carlotta Munny.

Who wrote *Grand Canyon Mishap*?
   Eileen Dover and Phil Lin.

What was J. K. Rowling's pen name?
   She didn't have a name for her pen.

Did you hear about the book on anti-gravity?
   It's impossible to put down.

What building in New York has the most stories?
   The public library.

What book has the most stirring topics?
   A cookbook.

How does a book insult a newspaper?

By calling it spineless.

Did you hear about the thesaurus factory that exploded?

Witnesses were astounded, shocked, surprised, startled, taken aback. . . .

Why can you always tell what Dick and Jane will do next?

They're so easy to read.

"But why can't I talk inside the library?" Mandy asked her mother.

"Because you have to be quiet. Noise is a distraction. The people around you can't read."

"Can't read? Then why are they at the library?"

5.
PLANES, TRAINS, AUTOMOBILES. . .AND OTHER WAYS OF GETTING THERE

. . . .

What is the only thing left after a train goes by?

Its tracks.

A man ran up to a farmhouse and pounded on the door. When the farmer came to the door, the man demanded, "Where's the nearest train station, and what time is the next train to the city?"

The farmer replied, "You can cut through my field, and you should reach the station in time for the 5:20. But if my bull sees you, you'll probably make it by 5:00."

A peanut sat on a railroad track.
His heart was all aflutter.
A train came speeding down the
track—*Choo-choo!* Peanut butter.

What is the difference between a
teacher and a railway engineer?
One trains the mind and the other
minds the train.

When does an automobile go exactly as
fast as a train?
When it is on the train.

Passenger: Are you sure this train stops
at San Francisco?
Conductor: If it doesn't, you'll hear
a loud splash!

Ed: How's your job at the travel
agency?
Ned: Terrible. I'm not going
anywhere.

A man boarded a train and said to the conductor, "I'm a heavy sleeper. Please be sure to wake me at 2:00 a.m. so that I can get off in Atlanta. Whatever I say, get me up. I have extremely important business there!"

The next morning, the man woke up in Richmond. He found the conductor and shouted, "Do you know how angry I am?"

"Probably about as angry as the man I put off in Atlanta," replied the conductor.

A woman boarded a bus for a ride into the city. The driver sped through the streets and changed lanes numerous times throughout the journey.

Not able to take it any longer, the woman stepped up to the driver and said, "I'm so terrified to ride with you driving, I don't know what to do."

"Oh, just do what I do," the driver answered. "Close your eyes."

Did you hear about the man driving in the country?

Where the road divided, his tire went flat. He had come to the fork in the road.

TRIPLE DOG DARE

A teenager told his father, "There's trouble with the car. It has water in the carburetor."

The father said, "Water in the carburetor? That's ridiculous. You don't even know what a carburetor is," he said. "But I'll check it out. Where is the car?"

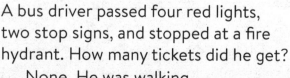

"In the pool."

A bus driver passed four red lights, two stop signs, and stopped at a fire hydrant. How many tickets did he get?

None. He was walking.

It was raining, the windshield was splattered with mud, and the car had almost collided with another vehicle twice. The hitchhiker was beginning to wish that this driver hadn't picked him up.

"Don't you think you should wipe off the windshield?" the hitchhiker asked.

"Oh, no," the motorist said. "That wouldn't do a bit of good. I left my glasses at home."

DOUBLE DOG DARE

A man was trying to pull out of a parking space. He first bumped the car behind him, then scraped the car in front, and finally crashed into a truck. A policeman arrived and asked to see his license.

"Don't be silly," the man said. "Who would ever give *me* a license?"

Two girls were reviewing the scene of an accident from which one had walked away unhurt the previous night.

"Wow!" the first girl said. "What exactly happened?"

The driver pointed to a telephone pole lying on the ground. "Do you see that?" she asked.

"Yeah," replied her friend.

"Well, I didn't."

A woman angrily jumped out of her car after colliding with another car. "Why don't people ever watch where they're driving?" she hollered. "You're the third car I've hit today!"

Why is the policeman the strongest man in town?
> He can hold up traffic with one hand.

What is round, sad, and lives in a car trunk?
> Despair tire.

What is the best thing to take when you're feeling run down?

The license plate of the vehicle that hit you.

A man went to get his driver's license renewed at the bureau of motor vehicles office. The line inched along for almost an hour until it was finally his turn.

He looked at his new picture for a moment and commented to the clerk, "I was standing in line so long, I ended up looking angry in this picture."

The woman beside him peered over his shoulder then said, "That's okay. That's how you're going to look when you get pulled over."

A man was trying to teach his daughter to drive. Suddenly she screamed, "What do I do now? Here comes a telephone pole!"

DOUBLE DOG DARE

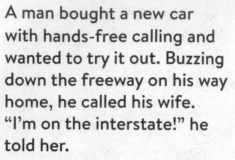

A man bought a new car with hands-free calling and wanted to try it out. Buzzing down the freeway on his way home, he called his wife. "I'm on the interstate!" he told her.

"Please be careful," his wife said. "I just heard on the radio that there's a crazy driver going the wrong way."

"A crazy driver?" he exclaimed. "No. . .there's *hundreds* of 'em!"

Two students were late to their first-period math final. They smeared some grease on their faces and hands and agreed on the excuse they would give. By the time they arrived at the classroom, it was empty. →

"We're sorry, Mr. Reese," said Greg. "We were on our way here and got a flat tire. We found the tire jack was missing, so we had to call for help. We finally got it changed and got here as soon as we could."

"Okay, you can come back tomorrow and take the test," the teacher said.

The next day, the students showed up to take the exam. Mr. Reese had the two students in opposite corners of the room and handed them each a piece of paper. The first question was very simple and worth ten points. The second question was worth ninety points. It read, "Which tire?"

A tourist was driving down a deserted road and came to a sign that said ROAD CLOSED. DO NOT ENTER. He thought the road looked passable, so he ignored the warning and continued driving.

A mile later, he came to a bridge that was out. The man turned around →

and drove back in the direction he'd come from. As he approached the warning sign he had recently ignored, he read on its opposite side, WELCOME BACK. TOLD YOU SO!

Martin had just received his driver's license. His family trooped out to the driveway and climbed into the car, as Martin sat in the driver's seat, ready to take them for a ride for the first time. His father was in the backseat, directly behind the newly minted driver.

"I'll bet you're back there to get a change of scenery after all those months of sitting in the front seat, teaching me how to drive," said the boy to his father.

"Nope," came his father's reply, "I'm gonna sit here and kick the back of your seat while you drive, just like you've been doing to me all these years."

"I don't think my right signal light is working," said Pam, stopping along the →

side of the road. She asked her brother Sam to check it, and he stepped to the rear of the car. "Try it now," he called. She pulled down on the lever and Sam reported, "It's working. . . . No, it's not . . . . It's working. . . . No, it stopped. . . . It's working. . . ."

One day a father was driving with his five-year-old daughter, when he honked his car horn by mistake. "I did that by accident," he said.

"I know that, Daddy," she replied.

"How did you know that?"

"Because you didn't holler at the other driver."

A woman pulled over at the policeman's signal. When he approached her car, he asked, "How long have you been driving without a taillight?"

"Oh no!" the woman yelled. She jumped out and ran to the back of the car. →

"Please calm down," said the officer. "It isn't that serious."

"But wait till my husband finds out!"

"Where is he?"

"He's in the camper that was hitched to the car!"

A man whose son had just passed his driving test came home one evening to find that the boy had driven into the living room. "How on earth did you manage to do that?" the man fumed.

"Simple, Dad," the boy said sadly. "I came in through the kitchen and turned left."

One day at recess, two boys noticed that a van was rolling down the school parking lot with no one in the driver's seat. They quickly ran to the vehicle, jumped in, and put on the emergency brake.

Seconds later, the van door opened and there was the principal, his face →

red with anger. "What's going on?" he asked.

"We stopped this van from rolling away," said one of the boys.

The principal, huffing and sweaty, said, "I know. It was stalled, and I was pushing it!"

DOUBLE DOG DARE

An insurance man was teaching his teenage daughter how to drive. Suddenly the brakes failed.

"I can't stop," she wailed. "What should I do?"

"Don't panic," her father said quickly. "Just hit something cheap."

What do you call the man who repairs bicycles?

A spokesman.

My poodle chases everyone on a bicycle. What can I do?

Take away his bicycle.

What is the hardest thing about learning to ride a bike?

The pavement.

A man went on a bike ride. He was speeding down a narrow, twisting mountain road. A woman, driving a car, approached from the other direction. She honked and shouted, "Pig!"

The cyclist was angry and grumbled to himself about a driver who obviously didn't want to share the road with bikers. He was still fuming as he rounded a corner and collided with a pig.

What is the best city to go bike riding in?

Wheeling, West Virginia.

Why doesn't a bike stand up by itself?

Because it's two tired.

What do you get if you cross a cactus and a bicycle?

Flat tires.

A man riding a bike and carrying two sacks on his shoulders was stopped by a guard while crossing the border. "What do you have in those bags?" asked the guard.

"Sand," the cyclist replied.

"You'll need to open them so I can take a look inside."

The guard emptied the bags and found out they held nothing but sand. The man put his bags back on his shoulders and continued across the border.

This happened a couple of times each week for a month. Sometime later, the same guard ran into the cyclist in the city.

"Hey, where have you been?" the guard asked. "You sure had me wondering. I know you were smuggling →

something across the border. If you tell me what it was, I won't report you. What was it?"

The man smiled and said, "Bicycles."

When is a bicycle not a bicycle?
When it turns into a driveway.

A small child on an ocean liner fell overboard. Before his mother could scream for help, a man quickly vaulted the rail, splashed into the water, and saved the child. The two were pulled back onto the deck and surrounded by cheering passengers. The captain said to the man, "That was amazing! What can we do to thank you for rescuing this boy?"

"Well," said the man, "you can start by telling me who pushed me overboard!"

What part of a ship is made out of cards?
The deck.

What do you throw out when you need it and take in when you don't?

An anchor.

Three brothers were in a small boat when a terrible storm developed. They were tossed overboard but able to swim to an uninhabited island. After two months, they realized they were not going to be rescued.

One day they found a magic lamp buried in the sand. They brushed it off, and—*poof*—a genie appeared. "I will grant three wishes," the genie said.

The first brother quickly said, "I want to be back home." He instantly disappeared.

The second brother longingly said, "I want to be back home too." And he instantly disappeared.

The third brother, realizing that he was now alone, sadly said, "I wish my brothers were back here with me!"

What do you get when you buy a boat at discount?

A sale boat.

From a passenger ship, everyone could see a bearded man on a small island shouting and desperately waving his hands.

"Who is it?" a passenger asked the captain.

"I have no idea. Every year when we pass by, he goes crazy."

How did the boat show its affection?

It hugged the shore.

TRIPLE DOG DARE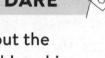

Did you hear about the red ship and the blue ship colliding?

The sailors were marooned.

For forty dollars, visitors to the county fair could ride in a barnstormer's biplane. An old couple who'd never flown before decided to give it a try, but the man grumbled about the cost.

The pilot offered, "Tell you what: you can ride together for only twenty dollars, as long as you promise not to scream or try to tell me how to fly my plane."

The old couple accepted the offer and climbed aboard. The pilot figured he could still get his forty dollars by giving his passengers a wild ride. But even through a series of loops and rolls, the pilot never heard a sound from the backseat.

"Well, congratulations," the pilot shouted over his shoulder as he landed the plane. "I thought for sure you'd be hollering when we made that nosedive."

"Oh, that wasn't so bad," yelled the farmer. "But I almost did break my promise a few minutes earlier when my wife fell out."

Upon landing, a flight attendant told the passengers, "Please be sure to take all your belongings. If you're going to leave anything, please make sure it's something we'd like to have."

A businessman was having difficulty lugging his oversized travel bag onto the plane. Helped by a flight attendant, he finally managed to stuff it in the overhead bin.

"Do you always carry such heavy luggage?" she asked, winded.

"Never again!" the man said. "Next time, *I'm* riding in the bag. My friend can buy the ticket!"

Bill: Did you tell Dan the new airplane joke?

Phil: Yeah, but I think it went right over his head.

After watching a news account of an airliner crash, a teenager asked his mother about the vital "black box" used in accident investigations.

"It contains a complete record of the plane's diagnostics right up to the instant of the crash," she explained.

"Why isn't it destroyed on impact?"

"Because it's encased in a very special alloy material, I'm sure."

"Then why don't they make the whole airplane out of that stuff?"

Before takeoff, a flight attendant made an announcement to the passengers: "Please let me know if you would like some gum before takeoff. It will prevent your ears from popping as we climb."

After the flight, everyone disembarked except one man.

"Do you need assistance?" the attendant asked him.

"Can you speak up?" he hollered. "I can't hear you with this gum in my ears!"

"I've never flown before," a nervous woman told the pilot. "You will bring me down safely, won't you?"

"Yes, ma'am," the pilot answered. "I've never left anyone up there yet!"

Four people were on an airplane—the pilot, a college professor, a pastor, and a Boy Scout. The plane suddenly experienced engine difficulty, and the passengers reached for the parachutes. However, they found there were only three parachutes on board. The pilot grabbed one and said, "I'm the most important man on this plane. I must go down and report this accident." He jumped out.

The college professor said, "I'm the smartest man on this plane. I'm working on a project that will be of benefit to all mankind." He grabbed a pack and jumped.

The pastor said, "Son, you go ahead and use the last parachute. I'm an old →

man—I've lived a good, long life. You go ahead and jump."

The Boy Scout said, "Sir, that won't be necessary. We can both jump, because the smartest man on the plane just jumped out with my backpack."

DOUBLE DOG DARE

A man jumped out of an airplane with a parachute on his back. As he was falling, he found his chute didn't work. He didn't know anything about parachutes, but as the earth rapidly approached, he realized the only way to save himself was to try to repair it himself.

The wind was whipping at his face as he rocketed downward. Suddenly, he saw another man shoot past him, →

going up. The jumper yelled, "Hey, do you know anything about parachutes?"

The guy zooming upward shouted back, "No! Do you know anything about gas stoves?"

A businessman was finally heading home after an extended trip. He presented his ticket to Seattle at the airline counter. As he waited, he asked, "Could you send the blue bag to Miami and the black bag to Houston?"

The agent, with a look of confusion, replied, "I'm so sorry, sir. We can't do that."

"Really?" he asked. "I am so relieved to hear that, because that's what you did to my luggage on my last trip!"

A woman walked up to the airline counter. The ticket agent asked, "Ma'am, do you have reservations?"

"Reservations?" she asked. "Of course I have reservations—but I'm going to fly anyway!"

6.
FATHER, MOTHER, SISTER, BROTHER. . .AND MAYBE AN UNCLE OR GRANDPARENT OR TWO

. . . .

TRIPLE DOG DARE

When I was little, my parents fed me a lot of alphabet soup.

They said I liked it, but I think they were just putting words in my mouth.

Lizzie: Mommy, Zach broke my baby doll.

Mommy: I'm sorry, sweetheart. How did it happen?

Lizzie: I hit him over the head with it.

One evening as a mother was preparing dinner, her seven-year-old son came down to the kitchen, crying hysterically. She bent down and said, "Honey, what's wrong?"

"Mom," he said, "I just cleaned my room."

"Well, I'm very proud of you," she replied. "But why on earth would that make you cry?"

Her son looked up through his tears and said, "Because I still can't find my snake!"

Mother: Kids, what are you arguing about?

David: Oh, there isn't any argument. Lisa thinks I'm not going to give her half of my candy, and I think the same thing.

A mother and her two small children, Zach and Lilly, were on a train ride to the city. Halfway through the trip, Zach →

asked his mother, "What was the name of the last station where this train stopped?"

The mother replied, "I don't remember. Why?"

"Well," the little boy answered, "because that's where Lilly got off."

DOUBLE DOG DARE

A mother was making pancakes for her sons, Jack and Chris. The boys began to argue over who would get the first pancake. Their mother saw the opportunity for a moral lesson. "If Jesus were sitting here, He would say, 'Let My brother have the first pancake; I can wait.'"

Jack turned to his younger brother and said, "Chris, you be Jesus!"

It was Palm Sunday, and Mary's four-year-old son stayed home from church with his father because he was sick.

When his siblings returned home carrying palm branches, the little boy asked what the branches were for. His mother explained, "People held them over Jesus' head as He walked by."

"I can't believe it," the boy said. "I miss one Sunday, and Jesus shows up!"

Mother: Hey, kids! We've saved up enough money to go to Disney World!
Daughter: Wow! When can we go?
Mother: When we have enough to get back home.

A young boy had been begging his father for a new watch. His father, getting frustrated, finally demanded, "I don't want to hear about your wanting a watch again."

At family devotions that evening, each family member was asked to share →

a Bible verse. The boy read Mark 13:37. "What I say to you, I say to everyone: 'Watch!'"

TRIPLE DOG DARE

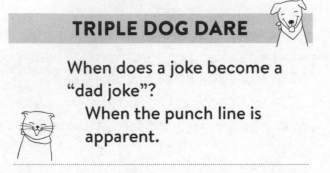

When does a joke become a "dad joke"?
When the punch line is apparent.

At a church dinner, there was a pile of apples on one end of a table with a sign that read Take Only One Apple, Please. God Is Watching.

On the other end of the table was a pile of cookies where someone had placed a sign saying Take All the Cookies You Want. God Is Watching the Apples.

Two kids went into their parents' bathroom and noticed the scale in the corner. "Whatever you do," said one youngster to the other, "don't step on it!"

"Why not?" asked the sibling.

"Because every time Mom does, she lets out an awful loud scream!"

My sister thinks I'm too nosy. At least that's what she keeps writing in her diary.

When do mothers have baby boys?
On Sondays.

A mother came inside after gardening and found a big hole in the middle of the pie she had baked that morning. She found a gooey spoon lying in the sink and crumbs all over the floor.

She went to find her son. "David," she said, "you promised me that you wouldn't touch the pie I made. And I →

promised you that if you did touch the pie, I would punish you."

A look of relief came over David. "Now that I've broken my promise," he said, "I think it would be all right for you to break yours too."

Mother: Jack, you're always procrastinating. You need to stop.
Jack: Sure, Mom. I'll change, I promise. I'll start Monday.

"I see our neighbors have returned our grill," the wife commented. "They've had it for eight months, and I was afraid that in their move, they'd take it with them by mistake."

"That was our grill?" shouted her husband. "I just paid twenty dollars for it at their yard sale!"

What do you get by putting ice in your father's bed?
A Popsicle.

Chase: My neighbors were screaming and yelling at three o'clock this morning!

Mark: Did you wake you?

Chase: Nah. . .I was already up, playing my bagpipes.

A father sent his boy to bed. Five minutes later, he heard, "D–a–a–a–d!"

"What?" he called back.

"I'm thirsty. Can you bring a drink of water?"

"No. You had your chance. Lights out."

Five minutes later, he again heard, "D–a–a–a–d!"

"What?"

"I'm thirsty. Can I have a drink of water?"

"I told you no! If you ask again, I'll have to punish you!"

Five minutes later came, "D–a–a–a–d!"

"What!"

"When you come in to punish me, can you bring me a drink of water?"

"Dad, is it okay to eat bugs?" the son asked.

"We shouldn't talk about bugs while we're eating," his father answered.

Later that evening, his father asked, "What did you want to ask me about at dinner?"

"Never mind now," his son answered. "There was a bug in your potatoes, but it's gone now."

Do you know that dads like jokes about elevators?

They work on so many levels!

A boy was visiting the zoo with his father. They were at the tiger display, and the boy's dad was explaining about how dangerous they can be.

"Daddy, if the tigers escaped and ate you—"

"Yes?" his father asked.

"How would I get home?"

Why did the child cross the playground?

To get to the other slide.

Two children were shouting at each other and were at the point of blows when Mom entered the playroom. "You two are always arguing," she scolded. "You need to learn to agree on things."

"We do agree," said one.

"Yeah," snarled the other. "We both agree we want the box of crayons right now."

"Ricky," his mom called, "last night when I turned out the kitchen light and went to bed, there were four cookies in the cookie jar. This morning there are only two. What do you know about that?"

"Well, it was kinda dark," Ricky confessed. "I only saw two cookies."

Mom: Where's your brother?

Sam: Well, if the ice is as thick as he thinks it is, he's skating. But if it's as thin as I think it is, he's swimming.

A mother scolded her son for not being fair with his little brother. "You need to let him have a turn with your skateboard," she said.

"Mom, I have," he told her. "I ride it down the hill, and he gets to ride it up the hill."

On the way to preschool, the doctor let his daughter look at his stethoscope. Her father thought, *Maybe one day she will become a doctor.*

But then he heard her as she spoke into it. "Welcome to McDonald's. May I take your order?"

DOUBLE DOG DARE

A little girl asked her mother for fifty cents to give to an old lady in the park. Her mother was touched by the child's kindness and gave her the required sum.

"There you are," said the mother. "But tell me, isn't the lady able to work anymore?"

"Oh yes," came the reply. "She sells candy."

A kind woman watched a small boy as he tried to reach the doorbell of a house. Thinking she should help, she walked up to the doorbell and rang it for him.

"Okay, what now?" the woman asked the boy.

"Run like crazy," he answered. "That's what I'm gonna do!"

A young girl was attending her first wedding, watching the proceedings with interest for a while before growing restless. The groom stood at the altar as six bridesmaids walked slowly up the aisle, one by one. Soon, the girl leaned over to her mom and whispered, "Why doesn't he just hurry up and pick one?"

Attending her first wedding, a little girl whispered to her mother, "Why is the bride dressed in all white?"

"Because white symbolizes happiness, and today is the happiest day of her life," her mother replied.

The little girl thought for a moment, then asked, "So why is the groom wearing black?"

Who is bigger—Mr. Bigger or Mr. Bigger's baby?

Mr. Bigger's baby, because he is a little Bigger.

7.
CHOWIN' DOWN

. . . .

What rises every morning but is not the sun?

> The bread in a bakery.

Why do bakers work so hard?

> Because they knead the dough.

Why was the bread dough sad?

> It wanted to be kneaded by someone.

Why did the doughnut maker retire?

> He was fed up with the hole business.

Why won't you ever find a lonely banana?

> Because they always stay in bunches.

What do you call two banana peels?
    A pair of slippers.

What kind of room does not have doors?
    A mushroom.

What is the worst vegetable to serve on a ship?
    Leeks.

DOUBLE DOG DARE

My sister bet me a hundred dollars that I couldn't build a car out of macaroni noodles. You should have seen her face when I drove pasta!

What do sea monsters eat for lunch?
    Fish and ships.

If fruit comes from a fruit tree, where do chickens come from?
  A poul-tree.

What is the best thing to put into a pie?
  Your teeth.

What do elves make sandwiches with?
  Shortbread.

What did the bread say to the knife?
  "Stop trying to butter me up!"

What are twins' favorite food?
  Pears.

I thought about going on an all-cashew diet, but then I realized, that's just nuts!

What do you call a fake noodle?
  An impasta.

What kind of bagel can fly?
  A plain bagel.

Why does everyone like it when the mushroom tells jokes at a party?
Because he's a fungi.

What do race car drivers eat?
Fast food.

Why didn't the police catch the banana?
Because it split.

Why did the pig become an actor?
Because he was a ham.

What did the cheeseburger name her daughter?
Patty.

My mom asked what vegetable I wanted with dinner. I said, "Beets me!"

Why did the cookie go to the doctor?
    Because it felt crummy.

What is orange and sounds like a parrot?
    A carrot.

Did you hear what happened to the peanuts walking down the street?
    One was a salted.

What kind of drink will give you a black-and-blue face?
    Punch.

DOUBLE DOG DARE

Why did the cup of coffee call the police?
    It got mugged.

What can you never eat for dinner?
    Breakfast and lunch.

What starts with T, ends with T, and is full of T?
    Teapot.

Why did the orange lose the race?
    It ran out of juice.

How do you fix a broken tomato?
    With tomato paste.

Why couldn't the coffee bean go out to play?
    He was grounded.

Why wasn't Jenny hurt when she fell into a puddle of Coke?
    Because it was a soft drink.

What fruits are mentioned the most in history?
    Dates.

What did the corn say when the farmer wanted to talk?

"I'm all ears."

Why did the other vegetables like the corn?

He was always willing to lend an ear.

What made the little strawberry cry?

Her parents were in a jam.

Did you hear how the cucumber became a pickle?

It went through a jarring experience.

What do you give a sick lemon?

Lemon-aid.

How do you make a milk shake?

Give it a good scare.

What is red when you go and green when you stop?

A watermelon.

How did the cheeseburger propose to his girlfriend?
  With an onion ring.

What did one plate say to the other plate?
  "Tonight, dinner's on me!"

118

8.
IT'S A SLAM DUNK TOUCHDOWN!

· · · · · · · · · · · · · · · · · · · ·

What dish do football players like to use for breakfast?

The super bowl.

The football team was losing badly. In desperation, the coach ran over to his worst player and said, "I want you to go out there and get mean and tough!"

"Okay, Coach!" said the player. He jumped to his feet and asked, "Which one's Mean and which one's Tough?"

Jax: Have you tried to shoot an arrow while blindfolded?

Max: No.

Jax: You don't know what you're missing.

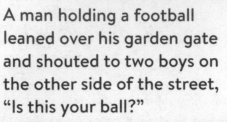

DOUBLE DOG DARE

A man holding a football leaned over his garden gate and shouted to two boys on the other side of the street, "Is this your ball?"

"Did it do any damage, mister?"

"No, it didn't."

"Then it's ours," said the boy.

There is an annual rivalry football game: big animals versus small animals. At the last game, the big animals were crushing the small animals. At halftime, the coach tried to motivate the small animals' team.

To start the second half, the big animals had the ball. On the first play, an elephant got stopped for no gain. On the second play, the rhino was →

stopped for no gain. On the third down, the hippo was thrown for a five-yard loss.

The defense huddled around the coach, who asked excitedly, "Who stopped the elephant?"

"I did," said the centipede.

"Who stopped the rhino?"

"Uh, that was me too," said the centipede.

"And how about the hippo? Who hit him for a five-yard loss?"

"Well, that was me as well," said the centipede.

"So where were you during the first half?" demanded the coach.

"I was having my ankles taped."

Why did the football coach go to the bank?

To get the quarter back.

What can be driven without any wheels and can be sliced without a knife?

A golf ball.

Why did the golfer wear two pairs of pants?

In case he got a hole in one.

TRIPLE DOG DARE

Brian and Randy were talking about their golf games. Brian said, "I got kicked off the course today for breaking sixty."

Randy was amazed. "Breaking sixty? That's incredible!"

Brian said, "Yeah, I never knew a golf cart could go that fast!"

What do hungry golfers eat for lunch?
    Their sand wedges.

Why do good bowlers play so slowly?
    Because they have time to spare.

Why should the bowling alley be quiet?
    So you're able to hear a pin drop.

What kind of dog hangs around bowling alleys?
    A setter.

What piece of jewelry do boxers always have?
    A ring.

How do you make a fruit punch?
    You teach it how to box.

What do baseball games and pancakes have in common?
    It all depends on the batter.

Why is a catcher's mitt like chicken pox?

Both are catching.

TRIPLE DOG DARE

Harry: What would you get if you crossed a baseball player with a Boy Scout?

Tom: I don't know, but I bet he sure could pitch a tent.

Where did the baseball player keep his mitt?

In the glove compartment.

Why don't matches play baseball?

One strike and they're out.

Why is baseball such a cool game?

Because of all the fans.

What would you get if you crossed a baseball player with a frog?

An outfielder who catches flies. . . then eats them.

Why does it take longer to run from second base to third base than it does from first to second?

Because there's a shortstop between second and third.

How do you stay in contact with a baseball player?

You touch base every so often.

What is the best day of the week to play a doubleheader?

Tuesday.

Why won't baseball players form a union?

They like to avoid strikes.

DOUBLE DOG DARE

A little boy was overheard talking to himself as he strutted through his backyard carrying a ball and bat and shouting, "I'm the greatest hitter in the world!" Then he tossed the ball into the air, swung at it, and missed.

"Strike one!" he yelled. Undaunted, he picked up the ball and repeated, "I'm the greatest hitter in the world!" When it came down, he swung again and missed. "Strike two!" he cried.

The boy paused a moment, examined the ball, spit on his hands, adjusted his hat, and repeated, "I'm the greatest hitter in the world!"

Again he tossed the ball up and swung at it. He →

missed. "Strike three!"

 "Wow!" he exclaimed. "I'm the greatest *pitcher* in the world!"

During a kids' sandlot baseball game, a spectator was surprised to see a dog walk out to the pitcher's mound, wind up, and strike out the other all-star team. Later, he would score two home runs.

"That's incredible," the spectator exclaimed to the man sitting next to him.

"Yes," the man said, "but he's a terrible disappointment to his parents. They wanted him to play football."

Why did the baseball player take his bat to the library?

Because his teacher told him to hit the books.

"Look, Billy," the coach said, "you know the principles of good sportsmanship. You know Little League doesn't allow temper tantrums or shouting at the umpire and other players."

"Yes sir, I understand."

"Good, Billy. Now, would you please explain that to your mother?"

Why did the kids start playing baseball at night?

Because bats like to sleep in the daytime.

Coming home from his Little League game, Bud excitedly swung open the front door and hollered, "Anyone home?" →

128

His father immediately asked, "So how did you do, Son?"

"You'll never believe it!" Buddy announced. "I was responsible for the winning run!"

"Really? How'd you do that?"

"I dropped the ball."

Jake: Oh no! I hit a run home!

Jared: Don't you mean a home run?

Jake: No, I mean a run home. I hit the ball through Mr. Wagner's window!

How do you figure a basketball player's salary?

Find out his net worth.

Why do basketball players eat doughnuts when they snack?

They like to dunk.

Where do basketball players go to press charges?

The court.

What are basketball players' favorite stories?

Tall tales.

Who was the basketball player's favorite poet?

Longfellow.

9.
SCHOOL DAZE

· ·

Karen: Are you in the top half of your class?
    Laura: No, I'm one of the students who make the top half possible.

The students in a kindergarten class were asking their teacher about her newly pierced ears.
    "Does the hole go all the way through?"
    "Yes."
    "Did it hurt?"
    "Just a little."
    "Did they use a needle?"
    "No, they used a special gun."
    Silence followed, and then one student quietly asked, "How far away did they stand?"

A third-grade class went to an art museum. Their teacher told them to sit and wait until the guide was ready to begin the tour. But two boys sneaked off to explore on their own. They walked down a hallway and entered a room filled with modern art pieces.

"Quick, run!" said one. "Before they say we made this mess!"

DOUBLE DOG DARE

Three friends were walking home from school.
"What should we do this afternoon?" said the first.

"I know," said the second, "let's flip a coin. If it comes down heads, let's go skating, and if it comes down tails, let's go swimming."

"And if it comes down on its edge," said the third, "we'll stay in and do our homework!"

A fifth grader was sent to the back of the line for being too rowdy while waiting to enter the cafeteria. He cautiously made his way back up to his old place.

"What are you trying to do?" asked the teacher. "I sent you to the back of the line."

"I went, but there's already somebody back there."

Principal: This is the fourth time you've been in my office this week. What do you have to say for yourself?

Sam: I'm *so* glad today is Friday!

Jeanne: Mom, I got a hundred in school today!

Mom: Good job! What did you get a hundred in?

Jeanne: In two things. . .I got a forty in math and a sixty in spelling.

What do history teachers talk about when they get together?

The old days.

A kindergarten teacher was having a difficult time putting each child's boots on after a very rainy morning. After some hard tugging, she finally got Barry's on his feet, when he said, "These aren't mine."

The frustrated teacher had to pull hard to remove them from the little lad's feet. She sat down next to him and asked, "So, whose boots are these?"

Barry answered, "They're my brother's, but my mom lets me wear them."

The father of a high school senior phoned the Latin teacher and demanded to know why his son had been given a grade of F on the midterm exam.

"Because we're not allowed to give a G," said the teacher.

What kind of food do math teachers eat?

Square meals.

Why did the teacher scold the student for something she didn't do?

She didn't do her homework.

Every year, the teacher sent a note home with each child that read, "Dear Parents, if you promise not to believe everything your child says happens at school, I'll promise not to believe everything he or she says happens at home."

What does a schoolteacher have in common with an eye doctor?

They both stare at pupils.

Why did the math teacher cry on the last day of school?

He hates being divided from his class.

What do English teachers eat for lunch?

Alphabet soup.

What did the history book say to the math book?

"Wow! You really have a lot of problems!"

Father: How did you do on your tests today?

Daughter: Okay, but on one I was like Washington and Lincoln.

Father: What do you mean?

Daughter: I went down in history.

Dad: Could you explain the D and F on your report card?

Son: No problem. It stands for "Doing Fine."

What did the colonists wear to the Boston Tea Party?

Tea-shirts.

Charlie: Hey, Mom, tomorrow there's a small PTA meeting.

Mom: What do you mean by "small"?

Charlie: Well, it's just you, me, and the principal.

TRIPLE DOG DARE

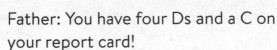

Dad: Why were you expelled from school?

Matt: I used a hose to fill up the swimming pool.

Dad: I didn't know the school had a swimming pool.

Matt: Well, it does now!

Father: You have four Ds and a C on your report card!

Son: I know. I think I concentrated too much on that one subject.

A little boy, who was doing his homework one evening, turned to his father and said, "Dad, where would I find the Andes?"

"Don't ask me," said the father. "Ask your mother. She's the one who puts everything away."

Where was the Declaration of Independence signed?
At the bottom.

Does England have a Fourth of July?
Yes. It's the day after the third of July.

Why did the boy go to night school?
He wanted to learn how to read in the dark.

The school board determined that speech and debate would be removed from the course schedule; there was no argument.

What is the worst thing you'll find in a school cafeteria?

The food.

What is the best state for school supplies?

Pencil-vania.

Why did the boy eat his homework?

His teacher said it was a piece of cake.

Why do scissors always win a race?

Because they take the short cut.

DOUBLE DOG DARE

What happened to the principal who fell into the copying machine?

She was beside herself.

Why is a bad joke like a broken pencil?
    It has no point.

Why is the library the tallest room in the school?
    It has the most stories.

Where do you go to learn how to greet people?
    Hi school.

"I have just developed the most powerful acid compound known to mankind," a scientist told her colleagues. "There is only one problem."
    "What is that?" asked one.
    "I can't find a container for it," she replied.

Why did the atom cross the road?
    Because it was time to split.

What travels faster, heat or cold?
    Heat, because you can easily catch
    cold.

Why was the wheel the greatest thing
ever invented?
    It started everything rolling.

What kind of table is in every school?
    A multiplication table.

Why did Benjamin Franklin like flying
his kite?
    He always got a charge out of it.

What makes math such hard work?
    All those numbers you have to
    carry.

Where were the kings and queens of
England crowned?
    On their heads.

Why were the early days of history called the Dark Ages?

Because there were so many knights.

What question must you always answer with a "yes"?

"What does Y-E-S spell?"

What ten-letter word starts with G-A-S?

Automobile.

What's in the middle of the world?

The letter *R*.

What eleven-letter English word does everyone pronounce incorrectly?

Incorrectly.

What is the longest word in the English language?

Smiles. There's a mile between the *S*'s.

How many times can you subtract four from sixteen?

Once. Then you are subtracting from twelve.

What did the calculator say to the student?

"You can count on me."

What do math teachers like to eat with their coffee?

A slice of pi.

Teacher: The law of gravity explains why we stay on the ground.

Chloe: How did we stay on the ground before the law was passed?

Teacher: What does N-E-W spell?
Student: New.
Teacher: That's correct! Now, what does K-N-E-W spell?
Student: Canoe.

TRIPLE DOG DARE

Mrs. Davis asked her English class, "Can anyone give me a sentence with a direct object?"

Zach raised his hand and said, "Everyone thinks you are the best teacher in the school."

"Why, thank you, Zach," replied Mrs. Davis. "And what is the object?"

 "To get the best grade I can," said Zach.

Teacher: What is the plural of *mouse*?

Student: Mice.

Teacher: Good. Now, what's the plural of *baby*?

Student: Twins!

DOUBLE DOG DARE

Miss Evans addressed her third-grade class after recess: "Did anyone lose a dollar on the playground?"

"I did, Miss Evans," said Rob. "A dollar bill fell out of my pocket."

"But this was four quarters," said Miss Evans.

"Hmm," replied Rob. "It must have broken when it hit the ground."

Teacher: Cathy, what would you do if you were being chased by a man-eating tiger?

Cathy: Nothing. I'm a girl.

Teacher: Correct this sentence. *It was me who broke the window.*

Joey: It *wasn't* me who broke the window!

A kindergarten teacher was showing her class an encyclopedia page illustrating several national flags. She pointed to the American flag and asked, "What flag is this?"

A little girl called out, "That's the flag of our country."

"Very good," the teacher said. "And what's the name of our country?"

The girl answered, "'Tis of thee."

The kindergarten class had settled down to its coloring books. Jonathon raised his hand and said, "Miss Franklin, I ain't got no crayons."

"Jonathon," Miss Franklin said, "you mean, 'I don't have any crayons. You don't have any crayons. We don't have any crayons. They don't have any crayons.'"

"Well," said Jonathon, "then what happened to all the crayons?"

Science teacher: What is the difference between electricity and lightning?

Student: We don't have to pay for lightning.

"Tell me," the teacher asked her third-grade students, "do you know what the word *can't* is short for?"

"Yes," said Lucy. "It's short for *cannot*."

"Very good. And what about *don't*?"

Matt's hand shot up. "That is short for *doughnut*."

Teacher: If I cut a steak in two, then cut the halves in two, what do I get?

Student: Quarters.

Teacher: Very good. And what would I get if I cut it again?

Student: Eighths.

Teacher: Great job! And if I cut it again?

Student: Sixteenths.

Teacher: Wonderful! And again?

Student: Hamburger.

At the beginning of math class, the teacher asked, "Ty, what are 3 and 6 and 27 and 80?"

Ty quickly answered, "NBC, CBS, ESPN, and the Cartoon Network!"

TRIPLE DOG DARE

A teacher had just discussed magnets with her class. At the close of the lesson, she said, "My name begins with M and I pick up things. What am I?"

Julia thought for a moment then answered, "Mom!"

What kind of cruise do college students travel on?

A scholarship.

10.
HOLIDAZE

Why do Pilgrims' pants always fall down?

  Because they wear their buckles on their hats!

Why wasn't the turkey hungry at Thanksgiving dinner?

  He was already stuffed.

How does the Easter bunny stay fit?

  Eggs-ercise.

What do you get by crossing a parrot and the Easter bunny?

  A rabbit who will tell you where he hid the eggs.

Why did the Easter egg hide?

  He was a little chicken!

Why did the Easter bunny miss the Easter Parade?

He was busy getting his hare done.

What is the Easter bunny's favorite kind of music?

Hip-hop.

Why is the Easter bunny the luckiest animal in the world?

He has *four* rabbit's feet.

TRIPLE DOG DARE

What do you call a group of Easter bunnies walking backward?

A receding hare line.

What is King Kong's favorite Christmas carol?

Jungle Bells.

Who was the smartest wise man?
The one with frankin-sense.

What is Rudolph's favorite weather?
Rein.

TRIPLE DOG DARE

What did the Gingerbread
Man put on his bed?
A cookie sheet.

What do you get if you cross Father
Christmas with a detective?
Santa Clues.

Who delivers Christmas presents to
dogs?
Santa Paws.

What do elves learn in school?
The elf-abet.

Which of Santa's reindeers is considered the most ill mannered?
Rude-olph.

What do Santa's beard and a Christmas tree both have in common?
They both need trimming.

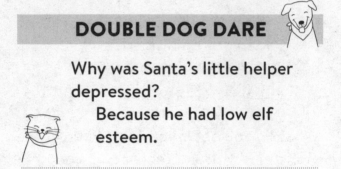

DOUBLE DOG DARE

Why was Santa's little helper depressed?
Because he had low elf esteem.

What disorder was Santa diagnosed with?
Claustrophobia.

Why did the Christmas cookie go to the doctor?
He was feeling crumby.

What is Santa's favorite outdoor activity?

Gardening. He loves to ho, ho, ho.

What kind of music do Santa's elves listen to while they work?

Wrap music.

DOUBLE DOG DARE

Why was Rudolph grounded after getting his report card?

Because he went down in history.

11.
THE WONDERS OF TECHNOLOGY

• •

A frustrated father was complaining. "When I was a teenager and got in trouble, I was sent to my room without supper," he said. "But my son has his own TV, cell phone, computer, and stereo speakers in his room."

"So what do you do to him?" asked his friend.

"I send him to *my* room!" the father replied.

Why was the cell phone afraid to go to the dentist?

She didn't want to lose her Bluetooth.

What did the baby computer say to the mom computer?

"Where's my Data?"

Television repairman: So, what seems to be the problem with your TV?

Woman: It has double images. I hope you guys can fix it.

How did the cell phone propose to his girlfriend?

He gave her a ring.

How does Bill Gates enter his house?

He uses Windows.

What did the mouse say to the keyboard?

"You're my type!"

What is a computer's favorite snack food?

Cookies.

What did the computer have for lunch?
Not much; just a byte.

What did the laptop do while it was at the beach?
It put on some screen saver and surfed the net.

TRIPLE DOG DARE

To the person who stole my copy of Microsoft Office: I will find you! You have my Word.

How do trees connect to the internet?
They log in.

Tech support: I need you to right-click.
Customer: Okay.
Tech support: Did you get a pop-up menu? →

Customer: No.

Tech support: Okay. Right-click again. Do you see a pop-up menu now?

Customer: No.

Tech support: Okay, sir. Can you tell me what you have done up until this point?

Customer: Sure, you told me to write *click*, and I wrote *click*.

DOUBLE DOG DARE

Why was the computer so tired when it got home from the office?
Because it had a hard drive.

Why don't computers eat anything?
They don't like what's on their menus.

How can you tell a good computer programmer from a bad computer programmer?

The good one always comes through when the chips are down.

How do you catch a runaway computer?

With an internet.

Why did the man turn on his computer on a hot day?

He wanted to open the Windows.

What's the first sign that a computer is getting old?

It has memory problems.

Why shouldn't you take your computer into rush-hour traffic?

Because it might crash.

Which way did the programmer go?
   He went data way.

Who is the best-paid employee at
Microsoft?
   The Windows washer.

12.
COPS AND ROBBERS, CRIME AND PUNISHMENT

Did you hear about the two hundred stolen mattresses?
    Police are springing into action to find the criminals.

What do you call the police chief's wife?
    Mischief.

Why was the police officer under a blanket?
    Because he was an undercover cop!

What does a policeman fly in?
    A heli-copper.

What did the policeman say to his stomach?
    "You're under a-vest!"

TRIPLE DOG DARE

Why was the belt sentenced to jail?

It held up a pair of pants.

Police officer: Where are you going?

Child: Running away.

Police officer: I've been watching you for ten minutes, and you keep walking around the block.

Child: Yeah. . .I'm not allowed to cross the street by myself.

Why did the policeman run across the baseball field?

A player had stolen second base.

Why did the police wake the child?

Because they had heard there was a kid napping.

Why did the picture go to prison?
    Because it was framed.

Why should you never trust stairs?
    Because they're always up to
    something.

What did the police do with the
hamburger?
    They grilled it.

A traffic cop pulled over a driver who
was speeding and asked, "Didn't you
see the speed limit signs posted along
the road?"
    "Officer," said the driver, "I was
going much too fast to read those tiny
little signs."

A truckload of hair picks has been
stolen. Police are combing the area.

A police officer discovered a perfect hiding place for watching for speeders. For several days, he caught several each day.

One day, everyone was under the speed limit, and the officer soon learned why. A twelve-year-old boy was standing a half a mile up the road with a large sign that read SPEED TRAP AHEAD. Just beyond the speed trap stood the boy's friend with a sign that read TIPS and a jar full of bills and coins.

DOUBLE DOG DARE

Police officer: Ma'am, you were doing eighty miles per hour!

Woman: Isn't that wonderful? I only learned how to drive yesterday!

A police officer pulled a woman over and gave her a speeding ticket.

"What am I supposed to do with this?" she asked angrily.

"Be sure to keep it in a safe place," he answered. "When you've collected four of them, you get to ride a bicycle."

A traffic cop in a small town stopped a motorist for speeding. "But officer," said the driver, "I can explain—"

"Save your excuses," said the officer. "You can wait at the jail till the chief gets back."

"But officer. . ."

"That's enough. The chief will take care of it when he gets here."

A few hours later the officer looks in at the prisoner. "Lucky for you that the chief's at his daughter's wedding. It means he'll be in a good mood when he gets back."

"Don't count on it," said the prisoner. "I'm the groom."

A man dialed 911, terrified after he was assaulted. "I was near my back door when I was struck on the forehead. Thankfully, I made it into the house and locked the door. Please send help!"

The dispatcher told him to stay calm then sent an officer to investigate. The officer soon returned to the station with a large knot on *his* forehead.

"That was fast," said the chief. "How did you figure things out?"

"It was really pretty easy," replied the officer. "I stepped on the rake too."

DOUBLE DOG DARE

What happened to the robber who stole the lamp?
He got a very light sentence.

What did the police officer say when he caught the woman who had stolen the office equipment?

"Just give me the fax, ma'am."

Three older ladies were driving down the highway at a very slow speed. A policeman pulled them over and explained that driving so slowly on the highway could be hazardous. The driver explained that she was following the posted limit: twenty miles per hour.

"Ma'am," he said, "that sign indicates that you are traveling on Highway 20."

"Well, that explains why Sally has been so quiet back there," the woman admitted. "We just turned off Highway 110."

How did the police know the photographer was guilty?

They found his prints all over the scene of the crime.

Judge: What are you charged with, Mr. Smith?

Smith: I was just trying to get my Christmas shopping done early.

Police officer: Yes—before the store opened, Your Honor.

Did you hear about the calendar thief?

He got twelve months; they say his days are numbered.

TRIPLE DOG DARE

"I am not at all satisfied with the evidence against you," said the judge to the man on trial, "so I shall find you not guilty. You are free to go."

"Thanks!" said the man. "Does that mean that I can keep the money?"

DOUBLE DOG DARE

Sherlock Holmes and Dr. Watson were on a camping and hiking trip. The first night out they had gone to bed and were lying looking up at the sky. "Watson," Holmes said, "look up. What do you see?"

"Well, I see thousands of stars."

"And what does that mean to you?"

"Well, I guess it means we will have another nice day tomorrow. What does that mean to you, Holmes?"

 "To me, it means someone has stolen our tent."

Inmate #1: So, what are you in for?

Inmate #2: Driving too slow.

Inmate #1: You mean driving too fast?

Inmate #2: No, I mean too slow. The police caught me.

Alex: Weren't you afraid when the robber pulled a knife out?

Will: No. I knew he wasn't a professional. The knife still had peanut butter on it.

Judge: I find you guilty, and I'm giving you a choice: fifteen thousand dollars or six months in jail.

Defendant: Your Honor, I'll take the money!

What is an inmate's favorite vegetable?

Cell-ery.

What is the worst name for a thief?

Rob.

Why did the thief steal an entire truckload of soap?

He wanted to make a clean getaway.

When is a crook neither right-handed nor left-handed?

When he is underhanded.

What do you call a group of convicts who go to the beach?

A crime wave.

How did they catch the crooks at the pig farm?

Someone squealed.

What do prisoners use to talk to each other?

Cell phones.

What do polite prisoners say when they bump into someone?

"Pardon me."

In the news: Earlier today, a police vehicle transporting prisoners collided with a cement truck. Officials are now looking for several hardened criminals.

How did the police search for the 6' 6" and 5' 2" prison escapees?
    They looked high and low.

What cafeteria food do detectives love?
    Mystery meat.

What case did the private investigator always doze off on?
    The pillowcase.

Why did the FBI agent spray his room with Raid?
    He thought it might be bugged.

What happened to the author at his trial?
    The judge threw the book at him.

A woman was found guilty in traffic court. When asked for her occupation, she said she was a schoolteacher.

The judge spoke from the bench. "Madam, I have waited years for a schoolteacher to appear before this court." He smiled with delight. "Now sit down at that table and write 'I will not run a red light' five hundred times."

How are a lawyer and an escaped prisoner similar?

They both had to pass the bars.

DOUBLE DOG DARE

What is a good name for a lawyer?

Sue.

13.
ALL GROWED UP

What joins two people but only touches one?

A wedding ring.

On their wedding day, a bride and groom were standing at the altar when she caught a glimpse of his golf club bag near the sanctuary exit.

"What in the world are you doing with those clubs at our wedding?" she asked.

"Well," he responded, "this isn't going to take all afternoon, is it?"

How do poets take their wedding vows?

For better or verse.

During her daughter's wedding, the mother of the bride kept from crying until the very end of the ceremony. But at that point, she noticed an elderly couple sitting a few rows back. The wife had reached over to her husband's wheelchair and gently touched his hand, and that was all it took to start the mother's tears flowing.

After the ceremony, the mother found the woman and told her how that tender gesture had made her tear up.

"Well, I'm sorry to spoil your moment," the elderly lady replied. "I was just checking to see if he was awake."

Sam: Do you spend much time wondering about the hereafter?

Ted: I'll say! Whenever I find myself in front of the refrigerator with the door open, I have to ask myself, "What am I here after?"

What did the bald man say when he received a comb for his birthday?

"Thank you very much. I'll never part with it."

DOUBLE DOG DARE

Fred noticed his life changed dramatically after he got a new hearing aid. Showing it off to his wife, he commented, "This is the world's best hearing aid. As a matter of fact, I can't remember hearing this well since I was a kid."

"Well, what kind is it?" asked his wife.

Fred glanced at his watch and replied, "Oh, it's about two fifteen."

Did you hear about the man who tried to swim across the Atlantic?

> He made it halfway across but was afraid he wouldn't make it, so he swam back.

Somewhat skeptical of his son's new excitement for fitness, the father took his teenager to the sports equipment store to look at the weight sets.

"Please, Dad," begged the boy, "I promise I'll use them every day."

"I don't know. It's a big commitment," the father told him.

"I know, Dad," the boy replied.

"They're not cheap, either," the father continued.

"I'll use them, Dad, I promise. You'll see."

Finally giving in, the father paid for the equipment, and they headed for the door. At the sidewalk, his son whimpered, "You mean I have to carry them all the way to the car?"

"My eighty-five-year-old grandfather gets up early every morning to jog two miles."

"That's amazing! What does he do in the afternoon?"

"The last mile."

While on a road trip, an elderly couple stopped at a roadside restaurant for lunch. After finishing their meal, they left the restaurant and resumed their trip. Unfortunately, the elderly woman had left her glasses on the table, and she didn't miss them until they had been driving about thirty minutes.

All the way back, the elderly husband scolded his wife.

They finally arrived at the restaurant, and as the woman got out of the car and hurried inside to retrieve her glasses, the man yelled to her, "While you're in there, you might as well get my hat too."

14.
THOSE GREAT OUTDOORS

· ·

Exhausted hiker: I am so glad to see you! I've been lost for three days!
    Other hiker: Well, don't get too excited. I've been lost for a week.

In which month do people exercise the least?
    February—it's the shortest month.

If two people can dig a hole in one hour, how long would it take for one person to dig half a hole?
    There is no such thing as half a hole.

What do snowmen have for breakfast?
    Frosted Flakes.

Why are snowmen so popular?
    They're just so cool!

What bites without any teeth?
    Frost.

What do snowmen wear on their heads?
    Ice caps.

What do snowmen eat for lunch?
    Iceberg-ers!

Where do snowmen go to dance?
    A snowball.

What do you have in December that you don't have in any other month?
    The letter *D*.

What is born in winter, dies in summer, and hangs from its roots?
    An icicle.

What was the most groundbreaking invention?
    The shovel.

DOUBLE DOG DARE

What do meteorologists call the end of a dry spell?
A rainy day.

Why did Mr. Twice tell his children to play outside during the thunderstorm?
Because lightning doesn't strike Twice.

TRIPLE DOG DARE

I recently took up fencing. But the neighbors weren't happy and asked me to put it back.

How many feet are in a yard?
It depends on how many people are standing in it.

What is the best way to cut wood?
    Whittle by whittle.

A man writing to the meteorologist:
"I thought you may be interested in knowing that I shoveled eighteen inches of 'partly cloudy' from my sidewalk this morning."

News anchor: So what's the chance of rain today?
    Meteorologist: Oh, no worse than 50 percent.
Anchor: And what's the chance you're wrong?
    Meteorologist: About the same.

Why did the thermometer go to college?
    He wanted to get a degree.

What tree is always unhappy?
    The blue spruce.

Where do walnuts look for their brothers and sisters?
    In the family tree.

What happens when trees are scared?
    They become petrified.

What is brown and sticky?
    A stick.

How do trees like to eat ice cream?
    In pinecones.

What is a tree's favorite drink?
    Root beer.

Which tree has the loudest bark?
    The dogwood.

What does a tree do when he is ready to go home?
    He leaves.

Which tree spends the most time on vacation?

A beech tree.

Where do you go to find information about trees?

The branch library.

What kind of tree is only found in a house?

A pantry.

What did the tree shout at the football match?

"I am rooting for you!"

One day, a young boy climbed a tall maple tree in order to gather acorns. After two hours, he still had not found any acorns. Why not?

Acorns don't grow on maple trees. They grow on oak trees.

Where do the baby trees go to school?
    At a nursery.

Why is a tree surgeon like an actor?
    Because he's always taking boughs.

Where did the gardener go for training?
    Nursery school.

What did one fish say to the other fish?
    "If you keep your big mouth shut,
    you won't get caught."

What is the best way to communicate with a fish?
    Drop him a line.

When is fishing not a good way to relax?
    When you're the worm.

What kind of flower grows on your face?
    Tulips.

What did the flower say to the bee?
  "Quit bugging me!"

What did the big flower say to the small flower?
  "What's up, Bud?"

DOUBLE DOG DARE

Why couldn't the gardener plant any flowers?
  He hadn't botany.

Why did the Martian get a ticket?
  He forgot to pay the parking meteor.

What can travel around the world without ever needing gas?
  The moon.

How does the moon cut his hair?
    Eclipse it.

Traveler: I'd like a ticket to the moon, please.
    Travel agent: I'm sorry, the moon is full now.

What did the launchpad say to the rocket?
    "Can I give you a lift?"

Why will the sun always get the highest grades in school?
    Because he is so bright.

How do the stars stay clean?
    They use meteor showers.

Why did the sheriff arrest the stars?
    They were shooting.

TRIPLE DOG DARE

Did you hear about the man
who sat up all night trying
to figure out where the sun
went when it set?

It finally dawned on him.

What can fall but will never break, and
what can break but will never fall?
Night and day.

Where do stars and planets go to
school?
At the universe-ity.

15.
SEE YOU AT CHURCH!

A Sunday school teacher asked her little students, as they were on the way to the church service, "And why should we be quiet in church?"

A little girl replied, "Because people might be sleeping."

A Sunday school teacher asked her class why Joseph and Mary took Jesus with them to Jerusalem. One little girl answered, "Because they couldn't get a babysitter."

Sunday school teacher: Why did Moses wander in the desert for forty years?

Olivia: Because he wouldn't stop and ask for directions.

A Sunday school teacher asked her children if anyone knew the first commandment. A little boy who was very sure of himself stood and said, "The first commandment was when Eve told Adam to eat the apple."

One day a teacher asked her Sunday school class to color a picture of something about the baby Jesus. Jimmy worked and worked and came up with a picture of a modern jet airplane with four people inside. The teacher couldn't quite figure it out. So she asked him, "Jimmy, that's a nice picture, but what is it?"

"That's Joseph, Mary, and baby Jesus on the flight into Egypt," Jimmy answered.

"Oh! . . . But Jimmy, there are four people in there. Who is the fourth one?"

"That's Pontius, the pilot!"

An eight-year-old boy was asked by his mother what he had learned in Sunday school. "Well, Mom, our teacher told us how God sent Moses behind enemy lines on a rescue mission to lead the Israelites out of Egypt. When he got to the Red Sea, he had his engineers build a bridge, and all the people walked across safely. He used his walkie-talkie to radio headquarters and call in an air strike. They sent in bombers to blow up the bridge, and all the Israelites were saved!"

"Now, Son, is that really what your teacher taught you?" his mother asked.

 "Well, no, Mom—but if I told it the way the teacher did, you'd never believe it!"

A Sunday school teacher was teaching the Ten Commandments to her preschool class. After explaining the commandment "Honor your father and your mother," she asked, "Is there a commandment that teaches us how to treat our brothers and sisters?"

Zane answered, "Thou shalt not kill."

A young boy came in late to Sunday school. He was usually on time, so the teacher asked him if something was wrong. The boy said he was planning to go fishing with his dad, but at the last minute his dad told him that he needed to go to church instead.

"Well, I'm glad you came! Did your dad explain to you why it's more important to come to church than go fishing?" asked the teacher.

"Yes," the boy replied, "Dad said he didn't have enough bait for the both of us."

A Sunday school teacher asked her class, "What must we do first before we can expect forgiveness for our sins?"

A little boy raised his hand and said, "Well, first we've got to sin."

A Sunday school teacher was telling her class the story of the Good Samaritan, in which a man was beaten, robbed, and left for dead. She gave the details so that her students would better understand what happened. Then she asked the class, "If you saw someone lying on the roadside wounded and bleeding, what would you do?"

One little girl said, "I think I'd throw up!"

"Now, how many of you want to go to heaven?" asked the Sunday school teacher. All the children raised their hands except one little girl.

"I'm sorry, I can't. My mommy told me we're going to Grandma's after Sunday school."

A little boy was sitting through the church service for the first time. As the usher passed an offering plate down his pew, the boy said, "Daddy, I don't think you need to pay for me—I'm under five."

DOUBLE DOG DARE

A young boy came home from church one Sunday with a chocolate ice cream cone. "Where did you get that?" asked his father.

"With the money you gave me this morning," replied the boy.

"But that money was for church!" said his father.

"I know," the boy replied, "but somehow they let me in for free!"

A young couple was visiting a church for the first time. As the preacher's sermon continued on, their little girl became restless. Finally, she leaned over to her mother and whispered, "Mommy, if we give him the money now, will he let us go?"

A minister received a telephone call from an IRS auditor who said they needed to discuss a tax issue.

"But we do not pay taxes," the minister said.

"It isn't you, sir; it's a member of your congregation, Jerry Williams. He noted on his tax return that he gave a donation of fifteen thousand dollars to the church last year. Is this true?"

The minister smiled and said, "The check hasn't arrived yet, but I'm sure I'll have it after I remind Jerry."

A preacher announced to his congregation: "I have good news and bad news. The good news is we have enough money to pay for our new building program. The bad news is it's still in your bank accounts."

TRIPLE DOG DARE

A young boy was invited to church by one of his friends. On the way out the door, his mother handed him two dollars. "One for you, and one for God," his mother said.

As the boy walked along with his friend, the wind blew his dollars out of his hand and onto the street. One of them went right down into the sewer.

 "Uh-oh!" the boy said. "There goes God's dollar!"

A crumbling old church desperately needed remodeling, so the preacher made an emotional request, obviously directed at the wealthiest man in town. At the end of the message, the rich man stood up and announced, "Pastor, I will contribute a thousand dollars."

Just then, a chunk of plaster fell from the ceiling and struck the rich man on the shoulder. He promptly stood again and said, "Pastor, I will increase my donation to five thousand dollars." Before he could sit back down, plaster fell on him again, and he quickly shouted, "Pastor, I will double my last pledge."

As he sat down, an even larger chunk of plaster fell, hitting him on the head. He stood once more and hollered, "Pastor, I will give twenty thousand dollars!"

At this a deacon shouted, "Hit him again, Lord! Hit him again!"

During Sunday school, the teacher wanted to see if the children would know what the Golden Rule was. The teacher said, "Joshua, can you tell me what the Golden Rule is?"

"Sure," said Joshua. "Do one to others before they do one to you."

"Does anyone know what the epistles are?" the Sunday school teacher asked.

"The wives of the apostles?" a little girl asked.

"Mommy, I learned the greatest miracle in the whole Bible today at Sunday school," a boy told his mother.

Expecting to hear about the parting of the Red Sea, one of the many miracles of Jesus, or the burning bush, the mother asked, "What was it, Son?"

The boy replied, "Joshua told his son to stand still. . .and he obeyed him!"

The Sunday school teacher told her class about the "children of Israel." She described how they crossed the Red Sea, defeated the Philistines in battle, and built the temple. Then she was interrupted by a young girl.

"So where were all the grown-ups?" she asked.

A Sunday school teacher asked her class, "What was Jesus' mother's name?"

One child answered, "Mary."

"Who knows what Jesus' father's name was?" the teacher asked next.

A little boy replied, "Verge."

"Verge?" the teacher asked. "Where did you hear that?"

"Well," the boy said, "you know they're always talking about Verge 'n' Mary."

DOUBLE DOG DARE

A Sunday school teacher was reading a Bible story to her class. "The man named Lot was warned to take his wife and flee out of the city, but his wife looked back and turned to salt."

A little boy asked, "What happened to the flea?"

The Sunday school teacher had just finished the lesson. She had taught the portion of the Bible that told of how Lot's wife looked back and turned into a pillar of salt.

Jeremy raised his hand. "My mommy looked back once when she was driving, and she turned into a telephone pole!"

Sunday school teacher: Phil, who was the first woman?

Phil: I don't know.

Sunday school teacher: I'll give you a hint. It had something to do with an apple.

Phil: Ummm. . .Granny Smith?

The Sunday school teacher was explaining the story of Elijah and the false prophets of Baal. She explained how Elijah built the altar, cut the bull into pieces, and laid those pieces and wood on the altar. Then Elijah commanded the people of God to fill four barrels of water and pour them on the altar. He had them do this three times.

"Can anyone tell me why Elijah would ask the people to pour water over the bull on the altar?" asked the teacher.

A little girl answered, "To make the gravy?"

The Sunday school teacher asked, "Tell me, do you pray before eating?"

"Nope," the boy replied, "we don't have to. My mom is a good cook."

A father was teaching his son to admire the beauties of nature.

"Look, Son," he exclaimed, "isn't that sunset a beautiful picture God has painted?"

"It sure is, Dad," responded the youngster enthusiastically, "especially since God had to paint it with His left hand."

The father was confused, "What do you mean? His left hand?"

"Well," answered the boy, "my Sunday school teacher said that Jesus was sitting on God's right hand."

Sunday school teacher: Now, Charlie, what can you tell me about Goliath?

Charlie: Goliath was the man David rocked to sleep.

TRIPLE DOG DARE

A man was lying on the grass and looking up at the sky. As he watched the clouds drift by, he asked, "God, how long is a million years?"

God answered, "To Me, a million years is as a minute."

The man asked, "God, how much is a million dollars?"

God answered, "To Me, a million dollars is as a penny."

The man then asked, "God, can I have a penny?"

God answered, "In a minute."

A little boy was praying at bedtime. "I can't hear you," whispered his mother. "I'm not talking to you," the boy whispered back.

DOUBLE DOG DARE

On the first night of his grandmother's visit, a small boy was saying his prayers. "Please, Lord," he shouted, "send me a bicycle, a tool chest, a—"

"Why are you praying so loud?" his older brother interrupted. "God isn't deaf."

"I know He isn't," replied the boy. "But Grandma is."

A four-year-old boy was asked to pray before dinner. The family members bowed their heads. He began his prayer, thanking God for all his friends and family members. Then he began to thank God for the food. He gave thanks for the chicken, the mashed potatoes, the fruit salad, and even the milk. Then →

he paused, and everyone waited.

After a long silence, the little boy opened one eye, looked at his mother, and asked, "If I thank God for the broccoli, won't He know that I'm lying?"

Minister: Son, faith can move mountains.

Boy: Yeah, but dynamite's more exciting!

A preacher, newly called to a small country town, needed to mail a letter. Passing a young boy on the street, the pastor asked where he could find the post office. After getting his answer, the minister thanked the boy and said, "If you'll come to the community church this evening, you can hear me tell everyone how to get to heaven."

"I don't know, sir," the boy replied. "You don't even know how to get to the post office!"

The preacher stopped in the middle of his powerful sermon to ask, "Who is God, anyway?"

From the back of the church, a little boy said, "God is a chauffeur."

"Why do you say that?" asked the preacher.

"Because," said the boy, "He drove Adam and Eve out of the Garden of Eden."

A young man stood staring at a large plaque hanging on the wall of the church foyer. When the minister approached him, the young man asked, "Sir, what is this?"

"Those are the names of the men who died in the service," the pastor replied.

The two stood quietly before the plaque for a moment. Then the young man broke the silence. "Which service? The 8:30 or the 10:30?"

TRIPLE DOG DARE

A pastor was visiting the home of a family in his congregation. Their little son ran in, holding a mouse by the tail.

"Don't worry, Mom, it's dead," he reported. "We chased him, then hit him until. . ."

Just then he caught sight of the pastor. He lowered his voice and eyes and finished, ". . .until God called him home."

The front door of a country family's home warped, causing the door to jam on occasion. To pry it open, they kept a hatchet handy.

One day the doorbell rang. Todd peeked out through the curtains and →

then shouted in a voice that could be heard through the door, "Quick, Kevin, it's the pastor. Get the hatchet!"

After a church service, three boys were bragging about their fathers.

The first boy said, "My dad scribbles a few words on a piece of paper, calls it a poem, and gets fifty dollars for it."

The second boy said, "That's nothing—my dad scribbles a few words on a piece of paper, calls it a song, and he gets a hundred dollars."

The third boy said, "I've got you both beat. My dad scribbles a few words on a piece of paper, calls it a sermon, and it takes ten people to collect all the money!"

A pastor, just out of seminary, was invited to speak at a chapel service in a prison. He was excited but a bit nervous as well.

When he arrived at the prison, →

he was greeted by a large group of inmates waiting to hear him. As the young pastor stood behind the podium, he said, "Good morning. It's so good that you're all here!"

After the sermon, a young boy had a question. "Pastor," he said when he saw him in the lobby, "I heard you say that our bodies came from the dust."

"That's right, I did."

"And didn't you say that when we die, our bodies go back to dust?"

"Yes, I'm glad you were listening," the pastor replied.

"Well I think you better come over to our house right away and look under my bed," the boy said, "'cause I think there's someone either coming or going!"

16.
KNOCK, KNOCK, WHO'S THERE?

Knock, knock.
Who's there?
Avenue.
Avenue who?
Avenue heard this knock-knock joke
before?

Knock, knock.
Who's there?
Lettuce.
Lettuce who?
Lettuce in—it's cold out here.

Knock, knock.
Who's there?
Juno.
Juno who?
Juno what time it is?

Knock, knock.
Who's there?
Warrior.
Warrior who?
Warrior been? I've been knocking for hours!

Knock, knock.
Who's there?
Dishes.
Dishes who?
Dishes me. Who are you?

Knock, knock.
Who's there?
Hatch.
Hatch who?
Bless you!

DOUBLE DOG DARE

Knock, knock.
   Who's there?
Amish.
   Amish who?
You're a shoe? Oh, okay.

Knock, knock.
   Who's there?
Juicy.
   Juicy who?
Juicy what I just saw?

Knock, knock.
   Who's there?
Candice.
   Candice who?
Candice door open or am I stuck out here?

Knock, knock.
Who's there?
Annie.
Annie who?
Annie way you can let me in?

Knock, knock.
Who's there?
Canoe.
Canoe who?
Canoe play? I'm bored!

Knock, knock.
Who's there?
Icon.
Icon who?
Icon tell you another one of these knock-knock jokes.

Knock, knock.
Who's there?
Nobel.
Nobel who?
Nobel, so I knocked.

Knock, knock.
Who's there?
Butter.
Butter who?
Butter let me in!

Knock, knock.
Who's there?
Tank.
Tank who?
You're welcome.

Knock, knock.
Who's there?
Safari.
Safari who?
Safari, so good.

Knock, knock.
Who's there?
D-1.
D-1 who?
D-1 who knocked!

Knock, knock.
Who's there?
Ears.
Ears who?
Ears another knock-knock joke for you.

Knock, knock.
   Who's there?
Repeat.
   Repeat who?
Who. Who. Who.

Knock, knock.
   Who's there?
Cash.
   Cash who?
I knew you were nuts.

Knock, knock.
   Who's there?
Lena.
   Lena who?
Lena little closer, and I'll tell you a good joke!

Knock, knock.
  Who's there?
Orange.
  Orange who?
Orange you going to open the door?

Knock, knock.
  Who's there?
Spell.
  Spell who?
W-H-O!

Knock, knock.
  Who's there?
Wa.
  Wa who?
Why are you so excited?

DOUBLE DOG DARE

Knock, knock.
Who's there?
Owls say.
Owls say who?
Yes, they do.

Knock, knock.
Who's there?
Adore.
Adore who?
Adore is separating us. Please open it!

Knock, knock.
Who's there?
I am.
I am who?
You don't know who you are?

Knock, knock.
  Who's there?
Alex.
  Alex who?
Alex-plain when you open the door!

Knock, knock.
  Who's there?
Nunya.
  Nunya who?
Nunya business!

Knock, knock.
  Who's there?
Beats.
  Beats who?
Beats me.

Knock, knock.
  Who's there?
Kenya.
  Kenya who?
Kenya play a game with me?

Knock, knock.
  Who's there?
Sweden.
  Sweden who?
Sweden sour chicken.

DOUBLE DOG DARE

Knock, knock.
  Who's there?
Art.
  Art who?
R2-D2.

Knock, knock.
Who's there?
Says.
Says who?
Says me, that's who.

Knock, knock.
Who's there?
Iran.
Iran who?
Iran all the way over here.

Knock, knock.
Who's there?
Luke.
Luke who?
Luke through the peephole and see!

Knock, knock.
Who's there?
Howard.
Howard who?
Howard I know?

Knock, knock.
Who's there?
Odysseus.
Odysseus who?
Odysseus the last straw!

Knock, knock.
Who's there?
A Mayan.
A Mayan who?
A Mayan the way?

Knock, knock.
   Who's there?
Tennis.
   Tennis who?
Tennis five plus five!

Knock, knock.
   Who's there?
Gorilla.
   Gorilla who?
Gorilla me a hamburger!

Knock, knock.
   Who's there?
Cereal.
   Cereal who?
Cereal soon!

LOOKING FOR MORE LAUGHS?

This hilarious collection of jokes, funny stories, riddles, and one-liners is sure to make anyone laugh. . .even you sourpusses! Perfect for 8–12-year-olds, *An Arkful of Animal Jokes—for Kids!* features chapters on more than 30 kinds of animals, from alligators to chickens, monkeys to skunkies, and snails to zebras.

Paperback / 978-1-64352-251-7 / $4.99

Find This and More from Barbour Books at Your Favorite Bookstore
www.barbourbooks.com

BARBOUR
kidz
A Division of Barbour Publishing